T0025035

THE SCIENCE OF BEACH FUN

BY R. L. VAN

CONTENT CONSULTANT
Qing Ryan, PhD
Physics Education Research Group
California State Polytechnic University, Pomona

Cover image: Science explains why certain objects can help people float on top of the water.

Core Library

An Imprint of Abdo Publishing
abdobooks.com

abdobooks.com

Printed in the United States of America, North Mankato, Minnesota
052021
092021

THIS BOOK CONTAINS
RECYCLED MATERIALS

Cover Photo: Serr Novik/iStockphoto
Interior Photos: iStockphoto, 4–5, 9, 24, 32–33, 39; Ron and Patty Thomas/iStockphoto, 7;
Mike Pellinni/Shutterstock Images, 10–11; Sergey Novikov/Shutterstock Images, 12, 43; Chayantorn
Tongmorn/Shutterstock Images, 16–17; Shutterstock Images, 21; Max Topchii/Shutterstock
Images, 22; Wavebreak Media/Shutterstock Images, 26–27; Jenya Pavlovski/iStockphoto, 28, 45;
Ken Wiedemann/iStockphoto, 35; Red Line Editorial, 36

Editor: Marie Pearson
Series Designer: Katharine Hale

Library of Congress Control Number: 2020948191

Publisher's Cataloging-in-Publication Data

Names: Van, R. L., author.
Title: The science of beach fun / by R. L. Van
Description: Minneapolis, Minnesota : Abdo Publishing, 2022 | Series: The science of fun | Includes
      online resources and index.
Identifiers: ISBN 9781532195174 (lib. bdg.) | ISBN 9781644946114 (pbk.) |
      ISBN 9781098215484 (ebook)
Subjects: LCSH: Beaches--Juvenile literature. | Force and energy--Juvenile literature. | Physics--
      Juvenile literature. | Dynamics--Juvenile literature. | Motion--Juvenile literature.
Classification: DDC 531.1--dc23

CONTENTS

AT THE BEACH

Tia and Marcus love going to the beach. Their family goes to the lake every weekend during the summer. There's so much to do that it never gets old.

The sun seems to shine extra brightly today. Tia and Marcus put sunscreen on. Then they start building sandcastles. Marcus wants to build a tall castle with a moat. Tia will build a small castle with lots of details. She even made flags at home to decorate it.

Building sandcastles is a fun family activity at the beach.

Tia and Marcus set up their buckets and shovels near the water. The sand here is wet, but not too wet. They pack sand into buckets and carefully flip them over. Marcus starts with a big base. Each level gets smaller as he builds higher. Then he digs a narrow moat. He connects it to the lake. The water flows around his sandcastle.

Tia carefully draws lines into her castle's walls. She doesn't want the sand to crumble. She drips watery sand down the other side for decoration. She builds small towers. They're perfect for her flags. When she finishes her castle, she looks at Marcus. It will be tough to decide what to do next!

BEACH BASICS

Beaches are strips of land along bodies of water such as lakes or oceans. The materials covering beaches, such as sand or rocks, are usually shaped by erosion. Erosion is the process in which water and wind wear down rocks

Erosion from the ocean can create steep cliff faces.

SHRINKING BEACHES

Some beaches are threatened by erosion. Erosion is often caused by weather systems. Rising sea levels are another threat. The ocean may rise to cover part or all of some beaches. Human construction can shrink beaches. Houses and businesses may be built on beaches. Sand and plants may be removed and replaced with concrete for buildings.

Beaches are important for slowing down storms coming from the ocean. Plants' roots help hold a beach's sand and soil together. Without beaches, waves could crash into the shore at full power. Beaches are also habitats for many plants and animals. Losing beaches could harm these living things.

and land. For example, waves may crash against rocks. They may break some of the rock down into tiny particles that become sand.

Tides, or the rising and falling of sea levels, are one of the main causes of changes to beaches. So are ocean currents, which are flows of water within the ocean. The moving water carries sediment. This material can include sand, shells, plants, and more. The water pushes the sediment onto the

Gentle waves can help build sand on a beach.

shore, creating beaches in a process called deposition. The water also pulls sediment from the shore and carries it elsewhere. This erodes beaches. Together, deposition and erosion shape beaches.

Different types of waves can affect what happens to beaches. Some waves are made when the water is calm. These are called constructive waves. These waves carry more sediment than they take away. They allow water to pull back from the beach. The particles of sand

The height of waves changes depending on the time of day and weather conditions.

and rock can settle and pack together. Then they stick together more tightly when another wave hits. The beach isn't eroded as easily. Other waves are stronger and more constant. These are called destructive waves. These waves carry more materials away than they bring in. The particles flow with the water and are carried away.

SANDY STRUCTURES

There are many different activities beachgoers can do. Science plays an important role in each one. Building sandcastles is one favorite beach pastime. Experienced sandcastle builders know that moist sand is important. Without moisture the sand won't stick together. But if the sand is too wet, the structures won't

stay standing. Knowing how water and sand interact explains why.

Water molecules are small particles that make up water. The molecules are naturally attracted to each other. They stick together. This causes surface tension in water. Surface tension is when molecules on the surface of a liquid pull together more strongly than molecules below the surface. The molecules take up as little area as possible.

Grains of sand won't stick together on their own. But when they get wet, water acts as a tiny bridge between the grains. The surface tension between water molecules on each grain of sand pulls the grains of sand together. This is why damp sand sticks together. But the sand shouldn't get too wet. If there is too much water, it will make the grains of sand slide easily against each other. The sand will flow with the water instead of sticking together.

Water helps sand stick together so people can shape it.

Sand will also stick together better if it is tightly packed. Packing the sand as much as possible helps shorten the bridges of water between grains of sand. This makes the connection even stronger.

Building sandcastles, swimming, and participating in water sports are all ways to have fun at the beach. Science can help people understand how all of these activities work. It can help people improve their skills. And knowing the science behind an activity can make it even more fun!

STRAIGHT TO THE
SOURCE

Renzo Piano is an architect, a person who designs buildings. In an interview with National Public Radio, Piano discussed his love for building sandcastles:

> For an architect to make something so simple, so easy, so playful, like a sandcastle, it's still about learning. It's about physical law, it's about intuition, it's about forces of nature—it's about understanding, at the end of the day. . . .
>
> But making something so useless like a sandcastle teaches you a lot about the responsibility of making something that must remain for centuries. I don't want to become too romantic, but in some ways, that's the whole point. You know, making something that will last half an hour is a kind of interesting opposite. It's a pleasure. It's taking up time, enjoying life.

> Source: "Blueprints before High Tide: An Architect Explains the Perfect Sandcastle." *NPR*, 1 Aug. 2015, npr.org. Accessed 16 June 2020.

WHAT'S THE BIG IDEA?

Read the passage above carefully. What's the main idea that Piano is trying to convey? How does Piano use details to support this idea? Write down two or three of these supporting details.

DIVING IN

One of the most popular ways to have fun at the beach is to go swimming. Wading in the shallow water, practicing swim strokes, and diving underwater all involve science. It all relates to the way the human body interacts with the water.

STAYING AFLOAT

Some objects, such as pool noodles, float in water. Others, such as rocks, sink. An object in water has two main forces acting on it. A force is a push or pull acting on an object. One force

Swimming and playing in the water can be great exercise.

is gravity. This pulls the object downward. The other main force is buoyancy. Buoyancy is the upward force that makes an object stay afloat in water.

Buoyancy is determined by a couple of different factors. One factor is the amount of water an object displaces, meaning the amount it moves out of the way. When an object enters water, it displaces some of the water. That water has to move somewhere else. For example, if an ice cube is dropped in a glass of water, it takes up space in the glass. The water that filled that space before the ice cube was added is displaced. The water level in the glass will rise.

The buoyant force is equal to the weight of the water that the object displaced. For an object to stay afloat, the buoyant force pushing upward must be equal to the object's weight. If an object displaces an amount of water that weighs the same as the object itself, then the forces of gravity and buoyancy will be equal. The object will float. If the object weighs more than the displaced water, then the pull of gravity will be stronger. The object will sink.

One way to determine whether something will float or sink is by looking at its density. Density describes how much space an object's mass takes up. Comparing the density of an object against the density of the liquid it is in will tell if the object will float. Water has a certain density. If an object is denser than the water, it will sink. If it is less dense, it will float. The material in a rock is packed very tightly. It takes up a small space. The rock is dense. On the other hand, the particles of the foamy

A BREATH OF FRESH AIR

When humans breathe, they take in oxygen gas from the air. They breathe out carbon dioxide. When people hold their breath, carbon dioxide builds up. If the levels of carbon dioxide in the body get high enough, a reflex will force the person to exhale. But when people are underwater, the body's diving reflex makes them able to hold their breath for longer. The body uses oxygen more slowly. This means carbon dioxide levels are slower to increase.

material in a pool noodle are packed loosely. They have air between them and are spread out. The pool noodle is less dense than water. This is why a rock sinks and a pool noodle floats.

These concepts help explain why some people can float in water more easily than others. Humans are made up of many different things, including water, bone, fat, and muscle. Muscle is denser than fat. So people with more fat can float a little more easily. The water a person is floating in also makes a difference. Salt water is denser than fresh water. So someone might struggle to float in fresh water but float easily in salt water.

GOING FOR A SWIM

Swimming isn't all about buoyancy. Moving forward in the water is part of the fun. This involves four main forces. The forces of gravity and buoyancy are two of them. The other two are drag and thrust. Isaac Newton's laws of motion can help explain how these forces work. Newton was a physicist and mathematician who lived

BUOYANCY

These images illustrate the different forces that make an object sink or float in water. Think about the way information is presented in these images. How does it compare with the way information is presented in the text? How do the images help you understand the text?

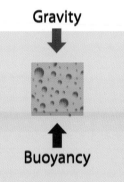

CORK

Lower density means gravity does not pull any more strongly on a cork than the buoyant force pushes. The weight of displaced water is equal to a cork's weight.

METAL

Greater density means gravity pulls more strongly on metal than the buoyant force pushes. The weight of displaced water is less than metal's weight.

The extremely salty water of the Dead Sea in Israel makes it easy for visitors to stay afloat.

in the 1600s and 1700s. He determined three laws of motion, which are three basic rules for how objects move. Newton's third law states that every action has an equal and opposite reaction. This means that if a person puts force on an object, that object exerts the same force on that person.

When a swimmer kicks or pulls water back, the swimmer is putting a force on water. That force is called thrust. It propels the swimmer through the water.

As a person's hands or feet push the water, the water in turn exerts that same force in the opposite direction. This pushes the swimmer forward. Additionally, when a person swims, that swimmer is pushing against the water ahead. According to Newton's third law, the water in front of the swimmer pushes back, slowing the swimmer down. This is called drag. Drag is a force that works against the motion of an object.

To move faster in the water, professional swimmers try to reduce drag. They do this in a few ways. One way is to wear special

SPEEDY SWIMMERS

Many fish are shaped in a way that lets water flow smoothly around them. Most can swim much faster than people. The sailfish is one the fastest-swimming fishes. It can swim faster than 68 miles per hour (109 km/h). Orcas are the fastest-swimming mammals, reaching speeds higher than 55 miles per hour (89 km/h). On the other end of the spectrum is the sea horse. It swims at approximately 0.01 miles per hour (0.02 km/h).

Special swimsuits and flippers make it easier to swim fast.

swimsuits and cover or remove hair. This reduces the friction that creates drag. Water can catch on hair and skin. This creates friction. Friction is the force of objects rubbing together and catching on each other, resisting movement between the objects.

Swimmers can also try to move in a way that helps the water flow smoothly around them rather than push directly against them. The freestyle stroke, or front crawl, is a good stroke for this. It uses the arms to cut through the water. Swimmers turn slightly to the side with each stroke, making their bodies narrower.

STRAIGHT TO THE
SOURCE

Engineer Timothy Wei uses his knowledge of the motion of liquids and gases to help swimmers move through the water faster. He says:

> *Thrust is what pushes the swimmer forward, and drag is the resistance of the water to the motion of the body. . . .*
>
> *[Swimming efficiently is] conceptually the exact same problem as . . . the design of an airplane. They put an engine on an airplane to push the airplane forward, and the air is resisting the motion. So the swimmer doesn't have engines. The engines are their body parts. And so they try and move their body parts in as efficient a way as possible to push water backwards. . . .*
>
> *You take advantage of all the different kinds of thrusts that are available to you, which is the arm motion and the kicking motion.*
>
> Source: "Missy Franklin and Fluid Dynamics." *NBC News Learn*, 11 July 2012, nbclearn.com. Accessed 16 June 2020.

BACK IT UP

Wei is using evidence to support a point. Write a paragraph describing the point Wei is making. Then write down two or three pieces of evidence he uses to make the point.

SURF'S UP

Surfing is an exciting water sport. People can surf in many different bodies of water. They just need a surfboard and waves. Warm ocean beaches are popular places to surf, but surfers can ride waves in colder places too. They can even surf on rivers or in lakes. Athletes need a good knowledge of wave science and physics to become skilled surfers.

SURF SCIENCE

Surfers wait for waves to come close to the shore. They paddle toward a wave as it rises.

A surfer paddles to find the right wave to ride. **27**

It takes a lot of concentration and balance to surf.

When the wave breaks, or starts to crash down into the water, surfers stand up on their surfboards. Then they ride the wave until it falls. The science behind surfing has some similarities to that of swimming. For example, buoyancy is an important part of surfing. A surfboard displaces a lot of water. The buoyant force pushing up on the board is equal to the weight of this displaced water. It's enough force to keep the board and the surfer afloat.

There are other scientific concepts at play too. When the surfer finds the right wave, the wave underneath raises her upward. This gives her potential energy. Potential energy is a type of stored energy, or the energy that something has the potential to use. As an object goes higher above the ground, there is more stored potential energy. For example, the higher something is when

WAVES OF THE FUTURE

Surfers can use weather forecasts to find good surfing waves. A forecast for a storm can give surfers an idea of the wind's strength. Wind helps make waves. There are websites designed to help surfers find the perfect wave. A website called Surfline employs meteorologists, or scientists who study the weather, to predict surfing conditions. They study winds over the water's surface, weather reports, data from buoys, and more. The website also has cameras set up so surfers can check on the waves at their favorite surfing spots.

it drops, the faster it will be traveling when it hits the ground. The higher the surfer gets raised up, the faster she will go after coming down. Moving back toward the ground turns potential energy into kinetic energy. Kinetic energy is the energy of motion. The surfer builds speed.

When the surfer is ready to slow down or stop, she shifts her weight back on the board. This tilts the front of the board upward. Meanwhile the back of the board is pushed into the water. It is at a more vertical angle against the water, so there is greater resistance against the flow of water. The back of the board pushes against the water. The water pushes back against the board. The greater resistance against the flow of water eventually stops the surfer's forward motion.

FURTHER EVIDENCE

Chapter Three covers the science of surfing. What was one of the main points of this chapter? What evidence was given to support this point? The website below goes into more depth on this topic. Find a quote from the website that supports this main point. Does the quote you found support an existing piece of evidence in the chapter, or does it add new evidence?

THE SCIENCE OF SURFING

abdocorelibrary.com/science-beach-fun

SEASIDE SPEED

Some of the most exciting beach activities involve high speeds. Whether the wind is giving an extra boost or a motorboat is cutting through the waves, these water sports use science to increase the thrill.

RIDE LIKE THE WIND

Surfing isn't possible at every beach. Some beaches don't get big enough waves. But another option allows people to take part in a similar activity without the waves. Windsurfing is a sport in which a rider stands on a board

Surfing is not an option on most lakes. Special kinds of boats create large wakes. Surfers can ride these wakes.

much like a surfboard. There is a sail attached. A windsurfing board is sometimes called a sailboard for this reason.

The sail and the wind acting on it are key to windsurfing. The sail is curved. Wind hits the sail. The air particles move more quickly along the outer curve of the sail. The air flowing on the outer curve of the sail has lower pressure. Its molecules are spaced out. Air in the inside curve of the sail has higher pressure. Its molecules are packed closely together. The higher-pressure air pushes against the inside of the sail. This push creates a force called lift. It pushes the windsurfer in the direction of the lower pressure, mostly sideways and slightly forward.

Since this lift direction is mostly sideways, it is very important to balance it with another force to the other side. To prevent the windsurfer from moving mostly sideways, the board is long and narrow. There is more

Wind allows windsurfers to ride across the water when there are few waves.

WINDSURFING AT WORK

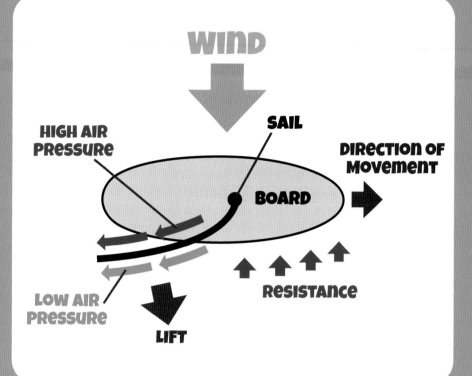

This image shows various forces acting on a windsurfer's sail and board. Compare the information in this image to the information about windsurfing in the text. How does the image help you better understand the text? What additional details are given in the text that aren't shown in the image?

drag if the board moves sideways than if it moves forward. It also has a fin underneath. The fin increases drag for sideways movement, but it creates little drag for forward movement. This allows the windsurfer to continue on a forward path instead of being pushed sideways by the wind.

Windsurfing boards and sails come in many different sizes. Beginners use larger boards. These help increase buoyancy and balance. They also use smaller sails. They aren't as heavy, so they're easier to move when turning. The windsurfer has more control.

TOTALLY TUBULAR

Trips to the beach often include boating fun. One boating activity is water tubing. This is an activity where

WINDSURFING SWANS

Scientists have found that a type of swan called the mute swan can windsurf. They windsurf by arching their wings over their backs. This pose allows their wings to work as sails. The wind pushes them across the water. Swans seem to be able to windsurf at approximately 3 miles per hour (5 km/h). When they just paddle along normally, they can go only 1.6 miles per hour (2.6 km/h). The scientists studying this behavior think the swans windsurf to save energy.

a person rides on a floating inner tube. The tube is attached to a motorboat. The boat tows, or pulls, the tuber along.

Inner tubes are very buoyant. Because they are made of light material that is filled with air, they have very low density. A tube floats and also keeps its riders afloat. The buoyant force pushing up on an inner tube is so strong that it would require a great deal of added weight to sink it.

Newton's first law of motion is important to the science of water tubing. It states that an object at rest or in motion will continue to stay at rest or moving with the same motion until another force acts on it. A boy is sitting on an inner tube. It isn't moving anywhere. To change the boy's current state of motion, a force has to act on it. The boat's motor moves the boat forward, pulling the tube along with it.

The tube moves in a straight line behind the boat. When the boat speeds up, Newton's first law says that

An inner tube can be pulled behind a boat at fast speeds.

at first the tube will keep moving at its original speed. The rope is providing the force to change the motion of the tube. Once the rope is pulled tight, the tube and rider will speed up. It takes a bit of time for the tube and rider to reach the speed of the boat. At first the rider will feel as if he is moving backward on the tube. This is similar to how people are pushed back into their seats when a car suddenly speeds up. The reverse

LIFESAVING GEAR

Life jackets can keep people afloat if they accidentally fall into the water. People also use life jackets during everyday swimming. Some life jackets have foam inside of them. This material traps air in pockets. Other life jackets are inflatable. They can fill with air or a gas called carbon dioxide. The trapped air or gas inside both kinds of jackets makes them very buoyant. Air has a much lower density than water. By trapping air, life jackets lower the overall density of the people wearing them. This helps people stay afloat. People already have some of their own buoyancy. They only need a little more buoyant force to float. The additional support from a life jacket keeps them afloat without needing to swim.

happens when the boat slows down. The rider will keep moving at the same speed. As the tube slows, the rider will feel as if he is rolling forward.

When the boat turns, Newton's first law says that the tube will tend to keep moving straight forward. But the rope connecting the tube to the boat will apply centripetal force. This is a force that pulls an object moving in a circle around the center of that circle.

Going to the beach is an opportunity to have fun. There are so many ways to play in the sand and in the water. Science explains why these activities are possible. Understanding the science of how beaches are created, how sand sticks together, and how water sports work can make the beach even more exciting. People can use science at the beach to find the best waves, improve their swimming speeds, and build the tallest sandcastles.

EXPLORE ONLINE

Chapter Four talks about Newton's first law of motion. The article at the link below gives more information on this subject. What information does the article provide about the first law of motion? How is the information from the article the same as the information in Chapter Four? What new information did you learn from the website?

THE FIRST LAW OF MOTION

abdocorelibrary.com/science-beach-fun

FAST FACTS

- Beaches are created through the processes of deposition and erosion. Waves bring sediment to the land and also remove sediment from the land.

- Sand sticks together when wet because of the surface tension between water molecules on grains of sand. Water molecules attract each other.

- An object's buoyancy, or ability to float, depends on the amount of water it moves out of the way when it enters the water. The weight of this displaced water is equal to the buoyant force that pushes up on the object.

- A swimmer moves through the water by generating thrust. The swimmer's arms and legs move the water away, and the water exerts the same force back, pushing the swimmer forward.

- Surfers build speed by using the potential energy of being high up on a wave. This energy converts to kinetic energy as they surf down the wave.

- Windsurfing sails move windsurfers forward because the air moves around the sail at different speeds on each side. The faster-moving air has lower pressure, so the higher-pressure air pushes the sail toward this lower-pressure area. The drag of the water against the underwater portion of the board prevents the windsurfer from only moving sideways.

Tell the Tale

Chapter Three of this book discusses the science of surfing. Imagine you are surfing on ocean waves. Write 200 words about your experience. What do you notice about the waves? What forces are acting on you?

Surprise Me

Chapter Two discusses the science of swimming. After reading this book, what two or three facts about swimming did you find most surprising? Write a few sentences about each fact. Why did you find each fact surprising?

Dig Deeper

After reading this book, what questions do you still have about the science of beach fun? With an adult's help, find a few reliable sources that can help you answer your questions. Write a paragraph about what you learned.

You Are There

This book describes how people float and swim. Imagine you are swimming in an ocean. How is it different from swimming in a pool? Be sure to add plenty of detail to your notes.

GLOSSARY

density
the amount of material in a certain amount of space

drag
the force acting against the motion of something in air or water

energy
the ability something has to do work, which is defined as moving something against a force

mass
the amount of matter in an object

molecule
a group of atoms, which are the smallest units of an element, that make up the smallest unit of a compound, such as water

pressure
the amount of force pressing on a certain area

surface tension
the tendency of molecules on the surface of a liquid to stick together

thrust
a force that pushes an object forward

ONLINE RESOURCES

To learn more about the science of beach fun, visit our free resource websites below.

Visit **abdocorelibrary.com** or scan this QR code for free Common Core resources for teachers and students, including vetted activities, multimedia, and booklinks, for deeper subject comprehension.

Visit **abdobooklinks.com** or scan this QR code for free additional online weblinks for further learning. These links are routinely monitored and updated to provide the most current information available.

LEARN MORE

Hestermann, Bethanie, and Josh Hestermann. *Marine Science for Kids: Exploring and Protecting Our Watery World.* Chicago Review, 2017.

Hutchinson, Patricia. *Boating.* Abdo Publishing, 2020.

INDEX

About the Author

R. L. Van is a writer and editor living in the Twin Cities, Minnesota. She has written nonfiction books on a variety of subjects. In her free time, she enjoys reading, doing crossword puzzles, and caring for her pet cats.